Two Nations

Two Nations

James Q. Wilson

The AEI Press

Publisher for the American Enterprise Institute
WASHINGTON, D.C.
1998

Available in the United States from the AEI Press, c/o Publisher Resources Inc., 1224 Heil Quaker Blvd., P.O. Box 7001, La Vergne, TN 37086-7001. To order, call toll free 1-800-269-6267. Distributed outside the United States by arrangement with Eurospan, 3 Henrietta Street, London WC2E 8LU England.

ISBN 0-8447-7112-0

1 3 5 7 9 10 8 6 4 2

THE AEI PRESS
Publisher for the American Enterprise Institute
1150 17th Street, N.W., Washington, D.C. 20036

Printed in the United States of America

Foreword

*T*he essay printed here is the lecture delivered by James Q. Wilson at the annual dinner of the American Enterprise Institute for Public Policy Research in Washington, D.C., on December 4, 1997. At that dinner, Professor Wilson received AEI's Francis Boyer Award for 1997—an award established in 1977 by SmithKline Beecham, in memory of its former chief executive officer, to recognize individuals who have made exceptional practical or scholarly contributions to improved government policy and social welfare. The Boyer Lecture series includes addresses by presidents (Gerald Ford, Ronald Reagan), statesmen (Henry Kissinger, Jeane Kirkpatrick, Alan Greenspan), jurists (Robert Bork, Antonin Scalia), and scholars (Thomas Sowell, Irving Kristol, George Will). Many of these lectures have proved to be of lasting intellectual importance; Professor Wilson's lecture, which was telecast live on C-SPAN and attracted considerable national attention and media commentary, is certain to endure as well. It is published here along with my introduction and tribute at the dinner. The lecture is also being published in the spring 1998 issue of *The Public Interest*.

James Q. Wilson was born in Denver, Colorado, and raised in Long Beach, California. He served in the United States Navy and earned his bachelor's degree from the University of Redlands and his Ph.D. from the University of Chicago. He was professor of government at Harvard University for twenty-six years (1961–

1987) and professor of management at UCLA for thirteen years (1985–1997). Among his many positions on government advisory panels, he was chairman of the White House Task Force on Crime (1966) and the National Advisory Commission on Drug Abuse Prevention (1972–1973) and was a member of the Attorney General's Task Force on Violent Crime (1981), the President's Foreign Intelligence Advisory Board (1985–1991), and the Board of Directors of the Police Foundation (1971–1993).

Professor Wilson's contributions to contemporary political scholarship and practical policy analysis are unsurpassed in their range and erudition. He is the author or coauthor of fourteen books, most recently *Moral Judgment* (1997) and *The Moral Sense* (1993) a study of the social bases of morality that one reviewer called "the most significant reflection on these matters since Adam Smith's *Theory of Moral Sentiments*." Among his earlier books are *City Politics* (with Edward C. Banfield), *Thinking about Crime, Political Organizations, Bureaucracy,* and *Crime and Human Nature* (with Richard J. Herrnstein). His *American Government,* now in its seventh edition (coauthored with John J. DiIulio, Jr.), is the leading college textbook on the subject. He is a frequent contributor to such journals as *The Public Interest, Commentary,* the *New Republic,* and the *Weekly Standard,* as well as to leading social science journals. Many of his essays on morality and human character have been collected in *On Character: Essays by James Q. Wilson* (1995), published by the AEI Press.

Professor Wilson is a trustee and chairman of the Council of Academic Advisers of the American Enterprise Institute and a director of several corporations and foundations. He has received numerous academic honors and awards, including the American Political Science Association's James Madison Award for a career of distinguished scholarship.

CHRISTOPHER DEMUTH, President
American Enterprise Institute
for Public Policy Research

Introduction

Christopher DeMuth

In 1987, when James Q. Wilson announced that he was retiring from the faculty of Harvard University at the age of fifty-five, a small scandal buzzed through the usually tolerant Harvard professoriate. It turned out that this renowned scholar and model of personal rectitude, who had received so many accolades and held so many positions of trust and leadership in his twenty-six years at Harvard, had a prior life: he had grown up in southern California. Moreover, it was then revealed that he and his wife Roberta had been California childhood sweethearts and were planning to run off together from Cambridge to . . . Malibu.

Harvard has since recovered its equipoise, but we now know that Harvard, and all of us, had all along been beneficiaries of Jim Wilson's *ausland* upbringing. For it was in Long Beach and Los Angeles in the 1940s that he first came to know, more palpably than anyone back East possibly could, where America was heading. It was there that he observed, and absorbed, the suburban, individualistic, freedom-and-mobility-loving, property-protecting, morally serious, politically skeptical ethos that was to become the defining political culture of America itself—prevailing through three wars, one near revolution, three economic booms, and huge ethnic and demographic changes. And I can prove he saw it coming at least as early as 1967, because he wrote in that year, in an essay drawing on his social roots and boyhood, that southern Californians

> are realizing their ambitions. They are . . . acquiring security, education, living space, and a lifestyle that is based in its day-to-day routine on gentility, courtesy, hospitality, virtue. . . . It is not with their lot that they are discontented, it is with the lot of the nation. The very virtues they have and practice are in their eyes conspicuously absent from society as a whole . . . the decay of values evidenced by crime in the streets, juvenile delinquency, public lewdness, and the like but going much beyond these manifestations to include everything that suggests that people no longer act in accordance with decent values and right reason.[†]

In this passage—written, I repeat, not in 1997 but in 1967—we see not only Tocqueville-like prescience but for Wilson himself a research agenda that would occupy him for thirty years, and a singular perspective to bring to that agenda.

His work is well known for its insistence and calm demonstration that social science for all its frailties really is a science, with greater practical utility in a wider array of public controversies than anyone had imagined. It can guide and improve policy in matters such as crime control and education where there is consensus on the proper ends of government. More surprising, it can help out with those fractious "values issues" of concern to the residents of Long Beach—issues of personal character and behavior, family structure, child rearing, drug abuse, welfare, even abortion—by clarifying the nature of our disagreements, settling disputes over causation and consequence, and suggesting policies that may partially unite warring camps.

Wilson is not, however, an academic imperialist: he knows the proper place of social science in practical affairs. Indeed, his

---

[†] "A Guide to Reagan Country: The Political Culture of Southern California," *Commentary* (May 1967), reprinted in *On Character: Essays by James Q. Wilson* (Washington, D.C.: AEI Press, 1995), pp. 75, 89.

latest book, *Moral Judgment*, argues powerfully against the use of social science findings in criminal trials, on grounds that true social science is concerned with tendencies, while the criminal law is concerned with judging specific conduct. And while many policy experts flatter themselves that their mission is, as they like to say, "telling truth to power," much of Wilson's career has been devoted to telling power to truth—that is, to explaining politics to the purveyors of abstractions.

Jim Wilson's earliest work in the 1960s concerned urban politics and policy. The problems of the cities—poverty, racial strife, crime, congestion, economic decline—were the central domestic issues of the day. America still had something like a self-conscious establishment, and its approach to those problems was managerial. "If we can put a man on the moon, why can't we solve the problems of the cities?" asked the editorial pages. The academy agreed and was eager to help. The field of urban studies was dominated by experts in city planning and public administration, who regarded politics as a nuisance at best. Wilson's fellow political scientists did not, but they saw the locus of city politics as the formal establishment, whether Brahmin or machine, firmly in control of City Hall and the civil service bureaucracies. And the political activists of the day believed the experts—the radicals reviling and attacking the city power structure, the liberals attempting to reform it.

But Wilson, and like-minded intellectuals such as Edward C. Banfield, Daniel Patrick Moynihan, Nathan Glazer, and Irving Kristol, said no: Government is not Management. Programs that attempt to solve urban problems through top-down management, like Urban Renewal and Model Cities, are bound to be fiascoes; and those that attempt to transform the establishment through bottom-up insurgency, like the Community Action Program, will add frustration to failure.

The all-powerful establishment, Wilson showed, was nothing of the sort, but just one—and a declining one—in a cacophony of competing ethnic, neighborhood, and economic interest groups. City Hall and the public bureaucracies only reflected the interplay of the competing forces they pretended to manage. Many urban problems were indeed serious, but they would not respond to the domestic equivalent of a war (as in War on Poverty) or a space program or a Marshall Plan. Any serious effort to ameliorate those problems needed first of all to recognize and accommodate the intensely political character of our government and the intensely pluralistic and competitive character of our politics.

That seems like a long time ago; the forces that disestablished the old city hierarchies have since done their work at the national level. The tendency to think and act as if society were a single organization with settled purposes is today much less pronounced—witness, for example, the disappearance of the idea of "fiscal policy," once regnant at AEI, Brookings, and the Council of Economic Advisers, which assumed that taxing and spending would be purposefully calibrated to maximize economic performance. Yet it still creeps in and confuses things every day. The most susceptible are the reformers of the Concord Coalition, Common Cause, Civic Journalism variety: high-minded people in sensible shoes who believe that if politicians would just stop being so parochial and shortsighted—or better yet would turn things over to an independent committee—all our problems would be easily solved. Asian-miracle journalists assure us that the Japanese and Koreans have already done so with great success, so we'd better get our act together, too (or at least they did until recently).

Partisan activists, who should know better, often succumb as well. Liberal Democrats today talk about organizing national child care in the exasperated, but-it's-just-common-sense tones of an 1890s Bellamy Club. Newt Gingrich announced on taking the Speaker's chair that what he was really going to be was CEO of the House. Is it any wonder that his supporters should be angry and confused that the CEO and his management team have not fully implemented their plans in three years, and have compromised, backpedaled, and shifted priorities in a manner that would be career ending in a business executive?

Professor Wilson teaches that it is not like that and never can be in a liberal, middle-class democracy where people's interests, experiences, and moral perspectives differ as much as in our own. On most political issues, we are obliged to make peace with people who are different, some of them very different, from ourselves. This does not mean that we are consigned to a multicultural Babel or advised to be muddle-through policy agnostics. To Wilson, pluralism and faction are not the end of the political question: they are its definition, the inescapable starting point for taking government policy seriously. We do face serious problems. Some of them are grave enough that they might destroy us. Such problems make the study of politics urgent and the arts of political leadership paramount—especially the moral imagination to define the problems at hand, and point to their solutions, in ways that appeal to the everyday experiences and sensibilities of large numbers of citizens.

It is on this latter point that Wilson has focused his most recent work, especially in his magnificent book, *The Moral Sense*. It is concerned with those issues of character, culture, and conduct that he noticed in Long Beach in the days of the Beach Boys and that have since become the most vexing issues of American politics. Our capacity for right conduct—meaning our inclination to discipline our immediate appetites and to act out of proper regard for others even when it is costly to ourselves— may be thought to be of divine provenance or to originate in an implicit, rationally self-interested social compact. But the immediate source of the moral sense is secular, explicit, customary, homey: it is in the organization of the family and the nigh universal practices of child rearing, where children are first taught proper regard for the interests of other family members, and those rules are then extended, partially and conditionally, to more distant social relations.

This formulation has profound political implications that have unsettled both strong libertarians and strong moralists. If Wilson is right, the continued success of self-government cannot be ensured by term limits, federalism, enterprise zones, or campaign finance reform: it depends critically on the fate of the traditional family. At the same time, morality itself is dethroned and democratized, revealed to be a popular art: it may be fortified by church and state but is ultimately in the hands of the most common and private modes of experience.

Libertarians and social conservatives have been quarreling with Wilson over theory and applications, but they have clearly been listening to him, and some have beheld a passage across the great current schism in political thought. Libertarianism is the right political philosophy for men and women who are equipped for liberty; but just as it breaks down where children are concerned, so, too, where adults persist in behaving like children. Social conservatism is right to insist that moral conduct is both definable and essential; but being good is not its own reward—it empowers men and women for freedom, with which they pursue happiness and achieve material and social progress.

In 1969, the first year of the Nixon administration, I found myself working in a White House that often seemed less like a center of government than an academic seminar, presided over by Professors Moynihan, Henry Kissinger, Arthur Burns, and George Shultz. Yet Pat Moynihan, who was in charge of urban affairs, kept insisting that President Nixon take time to meet with another professor, a Harvard colleague.

The president was resistant, offering excuse after excuse. Moynihan, of course, finally prevailed—performing that amazing physical feat since often observed but never successfully imitated. He pulled himself up to his full six-foot-four-inch stature *while still sitting down,* on the edge of his chair, and he said, "Mr. President, James Q. Wilson is the smartest man in the United States. The president of the United States should pay attention to what he has to say."

So should we all. The American Enterprise Institute's Francis Boyer Award for 1997 is inscribed:

To James Q. Wilson
Exemplary student and proponent
Of the American experiment in self-government
From its moral foundations to its practical operations
Which, he has shown, must be understood together.

Two Nations

W e live in a nation confident of its wealth and proud of its power, yet convinced that this wealth cannot prevent and this power cannot touch a profound corrosion of our cultural soul. We are materially better off than our parents but spiritually worse off.

The poorest Americans today live a better life than all but the richest persons a hundred years ago. But despite this great wealth, we inhabit, as Disraeli said a century ago, "two nations, between whom there is no intercourse and no sympathy; who are as ignorant of each other's habits, thoughts, and feelings, as if they were dwellers in different zones, or inhabitants of different planets." The two nations of which he wrote were the rich and the poor. But the great production and more even distribution of wealth that we achieved have altered the principle on which our nation is divided. Our money, our generosity, and our public spending have left us still with two nations, but separated by law and custom more than by wealth or favor. As Disraeli said, these worlds are "ordered by different manners, and are not governed by the same laws."

The American sociologist Elijah Anderson has put the matter more bluntly: In our big cities, the middle class, both white and black, thinks of itself as the outcome of the great tradition of Western culture, but nearby there is a second culture of young, marginally employed, sexually adventuresome, socially aggressive young men who reject the idea of hard work and social conformity that made their elders successful. For some, decent jobs are hard to find, but for at least as many others the effort to find and hold such jobs as exist has disappeared.

In one nation, a child, raised by two parents, acquires an education, a job, a spouse, and a home kept separate from crime and disorder by distance, fences, or guards. In the other nation, a child is raised by an unwed girl, lives in a neighborhood filled with many sexual men but few committed fathers, and finds gang life to be necessary for self-protection and valuable for self-advancement. In the first nation, children look to the future and believe that they control what place they will occupy in it; in the second, they live for the moment and think that fate, not plans, will shape their lives. In both nations, harms occur, but in the second they proliferate—child abuse and drug abuse, gang violence and personal criminality, economic dependency and continued illegitimacy.

Past Efforts at Reform

For decades our society has tried to make one nation out of two by changing everything—except the family. We have transferred money from the young to the old to make retirement easier and from rich to poor to make poverty bearable. Congress has devised community action, built public housing, created a Job Corps, distributed food stamps, given federal funds to low-income schools, supported job training, and provided cash grants to working families. States have created new approaches to reducing welfare rolls, and bureaucrats have designed affirmative action programs. We are still two nations.

Consider our efforts to rebuild families by training mothers to finish school and get jobs. When the programs were evaluated, not much had happened. The effects on the mothers were modest. Most stayed on welfare, and new pregnancies were not reduced. Even tougher programs have slight effects. When Florida imposed a two-year time limit on welfare, there was a small increase in employment but no reduction in welfare payments.

Our frequent bursts of good intentions have had little discernible effect on the central problems of our time. Bastardy has become more common, children more criminal, and marriages less secure. Much has happened, but little has changed. In 1950, 13 percent of the children born to teenage girls were born out of wedlock; in 1970, 30 percent; in 1990, 67 percent; and in 1994, 76 percent.

The family problem lies at the heart of the emergence of two nations. We wish people to work and to learn more in school. But there have been times in our history when unemployment was high and public schools barely existed. Yet in those days we were not two culturally opposed nations. Boys did not carry guns on the street, people were not shot for their expensive sneakers, drugs did not dominate our urban life, and students who had gone to school could actually read and write. Today, we are vastly richer, but the money has not purchased public safety, racial comity, or educational achievement.

The reason, I think, is clear: it is not money but the family that is the foundation of public life. As the family has become weaker, every structure built upon that foundation has become weaker. When our cultural framework is sagging, the foundation must first be fixed.

Importance of the Family

The evidence as to the powerful effect of this familial foundation is now so strong that even some sociologists believe it. Children in one-parent families, compared with those in two-parent ones, are twice as likely to drop out of school. Boys in one-parent families are much more likely than those in two-parent ones to be both out of school and out of work. Girls in one-parent families are twice as likely as those in two-parent ones to have an out-of-wedlock birth. These differences are not explained by income. Children in one-parent families are much worse off than those in two-parent families even when both families have the same earnings.

When the Department of Health and Human Services studied some 30,000 American households, it found that for whites, blacks, and Hispanics and for every income level save the very highest, children raised in single-parent homes were more likely to be suspended from school, to have emotional problems, and to behave badly. Another study showed that white children of an unmarried woman were much more likely than those in a two-parent family to become delinquents, even after controlling for income.

There is little point in dwelling on these facts; almost every American already understands them. Perhaps because of this understanding, the 1996 Welfare Reform Act is popular. But it is not obvious why our fears about families should make that law seem a solution. If implemented as intended, it will tell young mothers to be working, away from their children for much of each week. These children, already fatherless, will now not be raised even by their mothers.

But though changing welfare is popular, stigmatizing illegitimacy is not. Over half the public, and 70 percent of those under age thirty-five, think that no shame should attach to having an out-of-wedlock child. The stigma that once constrained bastardy has all but disappeared. Because of this, no one should be surprised that no matter how public policy has changed and the business cycle has moved, illegitimacy in the past three decades has increased.

William Galston, a senior White House adviser to President Clinton now teaching at the University of Maryland, has pointed out that you need only do three things to avoid poverty in this country—finish high school, marry before having a child, and produce the child after the age of twenty. Only 8 percent of children from families who do this are poor; 79 percent of children from families who fail to do this are poor.

Making a Real Difference

What is to be done? Social science, which for decades denied the importance of the family, may now have a partial answer. Everything we have learned in the past decade about the future of children suggests that the course is largely set in the earliest years.

I doubt that many parents would disagree. If you wish to make a lasting difference in a child's life, start very early and intervene quite massively. So popular has this idea become that it has been the subject of television specials and White House pronouncements. The results of these enthusiasms have so far been quite modest. But if early family life is crucial, little will result from installing V chips in television sets or giving tuition tax credits to the families of college students.

Let us begin with a few fundamentals. Children are not raised by programs, governments, or villages; they are raised by two parents who are fervently, even irrationally, devoted to their children's well-being. Although the benefits of two parents are beyond dispute, many children—in some communities, most children—are raised by one parent.

There is, however, evidence that early, intensive intervention can help even the children of single moms. It comes from small, experimental programs that have been competently evaluated. In Ypsilanti, Michigan, the Perry Preschool Project increased the chances that low-income children of welfare mothers would graduate from high school, gain employment, avoid teen pregnancies, and reduce criminality. In North Carolina, the Abecedarian Project found that poor children who received infant day care and family aid services did better in school tests.

These programs are much more intensive than what typically occurs in Project Head Start. In general, they involve child care, parent training, and home visitations. We are not certain why they are effective or for what kinds of children they are most effective. There are indications that they work best for the most disadvantaged children and least well for better-off ones.

We are also uncertain whether one feature of these programs, infant day care, helps or hurts every child. The most recent studies suggest that in general day care does not weaken the attachment between mother and child. But there is evidence that if the mother is doing a poor job of raising the child, some forms of day care may make matters worse.

We don't know whether programs that were successful in the 1960s or 1970s will be equally successful today in cities that have been devastated by drug abuse and gang warfare. And we don't know whether large-scale efforts will produce the same gains as small-scale experiments.

But even after allowing for what we don't know, the striking feature of the best of these small programs is that they produced large and lasting effects on children. They do not make children brighter, but they make them nicer. They may do this by forging stronger bonds to parents or inculcating a greater confidence in the future. And they do so more effectively than almost any program that tries to change grown children by altering their school experience, providing them with counseling, or sending them to special training programs.

Social science has also begun to suggest that a subject about which social scientists are notoriously reluctant to write—religion—has a significant effect, independent of economic status, in keeping children out of trouble.

Evidence has begun to accumulate that in the inner city, church-going males are less likely to commit crimes than are others of the same economic status. There is evidence, suggestive though not yet conclusive, that religious programs in prison reduce criminal recidivism for prison inmates more than what one would find among similar inmates in the same prison.

We do not know whether fostering religion in a child or supporting the youth-saving work of churches will produce the same effects that we now observe in the simple connection between religiosity and decency. But religiosity and decency are correlated; in time we may learn that the former causes the latter.

Enhancing Family Life

Let me suggest five things that might be done to enhance family life and thereby reduce the size of the underclass. Each idea is directed at one critical step in family life.

The Newborn Child. The infants of unmarried mothers require a home and truly adult care. Suppose that unmarried teenage mothers and their babies were required to live in a home under the supervision of experienced mothers. Some might be the mother's own mother, but many would not because their neglect has fostered their daughter's willingness to produce an illegitimate child. These young mothers would live in homes paid for with public funds but managed by private groups. No alcohol or drugs would be allowed. Boyfriends could visit only during approved hours. Every mother would attend school. Learning effective child care would be the central goal; staying off the street would be the central constraint. We would aim at teaching not self-esteem but self-respect.

One version of this approach is now in effect in Massachusetts. Called the Teen Living Program, it enrolls 120 teenage mothers in small residential homes. One is run by the Salvation Army, others by the YWCA, and another by the Crittenton Association. A girl can enter in the third trimester of her pregnancy. The average entering girl is fifteen; the average age of a child in it is two years. The girls can leave when they are eighteen and claim regular welfare benefits, but if they leave before they are eighteen, no such benefits are available. While in the program, the young mothers pay into the homes a portion of their welfare benefits and all of their food stamps.

The young mothers are selected because their own mothers cannot provide suitable shelters owing to child abuse, drug problems, or the like. Most of the children's fathers are older than the girls, and they rarely visit. Some of the girls don't like the rules and leave these homes, but others stay to the limit and come back as alumnae. The homes work hard at teaching girls how to be mothers, how to deal effectively with other people, why it is important to get an education, and how to cope with the temptation of drugs.

The program costs $38,000 per mother, and because the program is new, we don't know whether it makes a difference.

These two facts—high costs and unknown results—would doom this program for policy wonks. But it has one great attraction: it directs our energies at infants in the critical years of their lives, when a chance—perhaps the best chance, possibly the only chance—exists for saving them from reproducing the life of abuse and dependency that they would otherwise inherit.

Adoption. There are more parents seeking an adopted child than there are children to be adopted. Research shows that adoptive parents do a better job in raising children than do foster parents. Yet foster care survives, at high cost, while adoption languishes. The reason is the usual combination of bureaucratic inertia and misguided ideology. Most social service bureaucrats have no incentive to place an abandoned child with adoptive parents quickly, many are devoted to the discredited doctrine of family preservation at all costs, and some oppose transracial adoptions.

Foster care—which in many states costs more than $17,000 a year per child—makes little sense. And a good thing, too. The average foster child lives with three different families, and ten or more placements are not rare. Children remain in foster care to escape natural parents who are criminals, drug users, or child abusers. Meanwhile, thousands of American parents try to adopt children from abroad to avoid the miasmic sloth in which domestic adoptions are sunk.

There is an alternative, and Kansas has embraced it. It contracts with private firms to manage child care under a fixed-price model that gives each firm a powerful incentive either to restore the child to its natural parents or to find an adoptive home and to do it quickly.

The Preschool Child. If the lessons of the Perry Preschool Project can be generalized to many children, some combination of day care and home visitations may produce the same lasting benefits. We ought to find out.

Married Parents. Many need or want to combine a career with a child. To help, I suggest a plan designed by Richard and Grandon Gill. It would offer to a parent (typically, a mother) who wished to work the equivalent of the G.I. Bill of Rights. If you postpone your career and care for the child first—at least until it reaches school age—you will receive an educational benefit. It would enable you to finish high school, attend college or graduate school, or take technical training courses. People—chiefly, mothers—would be paid a public subsidy for discharging a vital social function. The gains to the recipient's earning powers that flow from greater education would partially compensate the economy—and through higher taxes, the government—for the cost of the subsidy.

Restoring the Force of Religion. Religion, independent of social class, reduces deviance. It lies at the heart of programs such as Alcoholics Anonymous, an extraordinary success that no government could have produced and no business could have sold. Hundreds of churches and synagogues across the country already try to produce better people out of discarded humans. Many provide aid to unmarried mothers, picket crack houses, recruit boys into anticrime activities, and require men to acknowledge the paternity of their children.

It is hard to raise money for religious programs. The government worries about church-state issues that the Supreme Court, without historical warrant, has imposed on it. And when the government does give money to churches, it often attaches to every federal dollar its full litany of rules, demands, and oversight. Business firms do not ordinarily give money to churches at all. Many would rather spend it on associations that attack capitalism.

There are good preachers and bad preachers, church programs that work and ones that do not. We have no way of finding out which is which save by intense personal inquiry.

We need privately funded groups that would evaluate the

fiscal soundness and programmatic intensity of church efforts, distribute to firms and foundations lists of apparently worthwhile programs, and help raise money for ones that pass this initial screening. We need in each large city the religious equivalent of the United Fund, but one that, unlike the fund, is focused chiefly on solving the problems of the underclass with church-related activities. Corporate funds would support the healing role of churches.

The policies I have described cost money and have unknown effects. How can I advocate spending more money on things about which we know so little?

In a rational world we would take money back from failed programs. Despite the absence of any evidence that federal spending helps schools, the federal government spends more than $6 billion a year on schools. Federal job training programs have, at best, modest effects; cut back on them. Nicholas Eberstadt of the American Enterprise Institute has calculated that in 1992 we spent $290 billion on persons with low incomes—$5,600 for every man, woman, and child in the lowest fifth of the nation's income ladder. Money exists, but this is a political world, and wasted money is rarely recaptured. But even if more money is required, recall the message of John DiIulio: if you find a man with a knife in his back, you don't make him better just by pulling the knife out. The American people have rejected the welfare state, not because it costs too much but because it has not helped people.

Beyond the Therapeutic State

Our goal is not to enlarge the welfare system but to change it. All about us lies the wreckage of the therapeutic state. It has created not self-respect but social dependency. When asked what the government should do to change family structure, Senator Moynihan answered this way: if you expect a government program to change families, you know more about government than I do. Governments can transfer money; they cannot build character. Our best hope is to transfer the money to private agencies—churches and other voluntary associations—that have shown in the past a capacity to change people.

The tougher question is what will work. Will anything I have suggested make a difference? I do not know, but these policies are consistent with what every parent already knows and what social science belatedly recognizes. The human personality emerges early; if it is to be shaped, it must be shaped early. Investing in early childhood is the most important investment any society can make. We have known that for centuries, but only in modern times have we led many parents—and by money subsidies, encouraged some parents—to avoid making this investment.

No parent, whether father or mother, can have it all. Choices must be made between family and work. The first must take priority over the second. This choice affects women more profoundly than men because women are closer to their children. The vast majority of all single-parent homes are female headed. This is not the result of a legal arrangement but of human choice.

If we care about how children are raised in their early years, and if, as is now the case, how they are raised is left to overwhelmed women or institutional arrangements, the only way we can restore the balance is by committing money to the task of inducing actions that were once the product of spontaneous choice.

Religion shapes lives in every culture that has ever existed and does so more powerfully than the mass media or government programs. Throughout the Western world, political and intellectual elites have abandoned interest in, or acquired a deep hostility to, the force that has given meaning to Western life. To a degree, this was understandable. The Enlightenment, of which we all are part, was created by thinkers who wished to end religious warfare and sectarian authority. But we have done more than end religious warfare; we have tried hard to end religion itself, thereby subjecting much of mankind to a new form of warfare—the hopeless struggle of lonely souls against impulses they can neither understand nor control.

This is a feature of almost all the Western world, and it helps explain why crime rates and illegitimate births have been rising rapidly almost everywhere and not just here.

Restoring a Culture

We live today with the advantages of three centuries of political and intellectual emancipation, but those advantages were purchased at a price. Most of us do not feel that price because we have transformed the teachings of the Enlightenment into personal wealth, political power, social advantage, or intellectual accomplishment. Those who have done so are part of one nation, proud of what freedom has allowed us to achieve.

But there is a second nation, growing more rapidly than the first. It is the nation that has paid heavily the high price of freedom. It is armed to the teeth, excited by drugs, preoccupied with respect, and indifferent to the future. Its children crowd our schools and fill our streets, armed and dangerous.

Cultures grow up out of the countless small choices of millions of people. To restore a culture, we must do it retail, not wholesale. We are not fighting the Second World War; we are trying to retake a captured city where the struggle goes on person by person, block by block, building by building.

That struggle may be lost. When a culture changes, policy can rarely change it back. But I am an optimist. America has been told that it would be destroyed by slavery, alcohol, subversion, immigration, civil war, economic collapse, and atom bombs, and it has survived them all. Most people wish to be part of one family and one nation. If we wish to be one nation again, we must make the second one part of the first. We have tried almost everything to do this except the one thing that matters most—rebuilding the family. However difficult, it is what there is left to try.

Sam Peltzman
Sears Roebuck Professor of
  Economics and Financial Services
University of Chicago Graduate
  School of Business

Nelson W. Polsby
Professor of Political Science
University of California at Berkeley

George L. Priest
John M. Olin Professor of Law and
  Economics
Yale Law School

Thomas Sowell
Senior Fellow
Hoover Institution
Stanford University

Murray L. Weidenbaum
Mallinckrodt Distinguished
  University Professor
Washington University

Richard J. Zeckhauser
Frank Ramsey Professor of Political
  Economy
Kennedy School of Government
Harvard University

Research Staff

Leon Aron
Resident Scholar

Claude E. Barfield
Resident Scholar; Director, Science
  and Technology Policy Studies

Cynthia A. Beltz
Research Fellow

Walter Berns
Resident Scholar

Douglas J. Besharov
Resident Scholar

Robert H. Bork
John M. Olin Scholar in Legal Studies

Karlyn Bowman
Resident Fellow

Kenneth Brown
Visiting Fellow

John E. Calfee
Resident Scholar

Lynne V. Cheney
Senior Fellow

Dinesh D'Souza
John M. Olin Research Fellow

Nicholas N. Eberstadt
Visiting Scholar

Mark Falcoff
Resident Scholar

Gerald R. Ford
Distinguished Fellow

Murray F. Foss
Visiting Scholar

Michael Fumento
Resident Fellow

Diana Furchtgott-Roth
Assistant to the President and
  Resident Fellow

Suzanne Garment
Resident Scholar

Jeffrey Gedmin
Research Fellow

James K. Glassman
DeWitt Wallace–Reader's Digest
  Fellow

Robert A. Goldwin
Resident Scholar

Mark Groombridge
Abramson Fellow; Associate Director,
  Asian Studies

Robert W. Hahn
Resident Scholar

Kevin Hassett
Resident Scholar

Robert B. Helms
Resident Scholar; Director, Health
  Policy Studies

R. Glenn Hubbard
Visiting Scholar

James D. Johnston
Resident Fellow

Jeane J. Kirkpatrick
Senior Fellow; Director, Foreign
  and Defense Policy Studies

Marvin H. Kosters
Resident Scholar; Director,
  Economic Policy Studies

Irving Kristol
John M. Olin Distinguished Fellow

Dana Lane
Director of Publications

Michael A. Ledeen
Freedom Scholar

James Lilley
Resident Fellow

Clarisa Long
Abramson Fellow

Lawrence Lindsey
Arthur F. Burns Scholar in Economics

John H. Makin
Resident Scholar; Director, Fiscal
  Policy Studies

Allan H. Meltzer
Visiting Scholar

Joshua Muravchik
Resident Scholar

Charles Murray
Bradley Fellow

Michael Novak
George F. Jewett Scholar in Religion,
  Philosophy, and Public Policy;
  Director, Social and Political Studies

Norman J. Ornstein
Resident Scholar

Richard N. Perle
Resident Fellow

William Schneider
Resident Scholar

William Shew
Visiting Scholar

J. Gregory Sidak
F. K. Weyerhaeuser Fellow

Christina Hoff Sommers
W. H. Brady, Jr., Fellow

Herbert Stein
Senior Fellow

Irwin M. Stelzer
Resident Scholar; Director,
  Regulatory Policy Studies

Daniel Troy
Associate Scholar

Arthur Waldron
Director, Asian Studies

W. Allen Wallis
Resident Scholar

Ben J. Wattenberg
Senior Fellow

Carolyn L. Weaver
Resident Scholar; Director, Social
  Security and Pension Studies

Karl Zinsmeister
J. B. Fuqua Fellow; Editor, *The
  American Enterprise*